What's for dinner?
Meal Ideas...

Paul Brodel and Dee Hunwicks

I would like to dedicate this book to my Mum (Linda), my Dad (Ted), and my Gran (Doris) who, from an early age, encouraged and supported me to follow my dream and passion for cooking.

Paul

I would like to make my dedication to my late parents, Celia and "Siddy" Howard, my wonderful husband Steve and my children, Darren and Hayley - who have always made me very proud. Also, to all my friends who have supported me through good times and bad, especially Uncle Paul, Val and Peggy. Thank you.

Dee

CONTENTS

FOREWORD

by Dee Hunwicks

There seem to be more copies of complicated recipe books on the shelves of libraries, bookshops and supermarkets nowadays, than there have ever been before. However, not everyone has the time, means or the inclination to trek to a specialist food outlet for the ingredients needed, hence the birth of "What's For Dinner? Meal Ideas". Our aim is to go back to basics. Whether all you have is a pack of minced beef for supper, or you want to create something special for a dinner party, we promise you'll find what you need in the following pages.

The man behind this wonderful idea is renowned television chef, Mr Paul Brodel and I'm Dee Hunwicks. I have the privilege of working alongside Paul in testing products and preparing food for his shows. Paul was born in Plymouth and has loved food for as long as he can remember. When he was young Paul sailed around the world with his parents and so was introduced to an array of new and exciting cuisine from a very early age. He also learnt how to create a meal in a tiny galley kitchen, with very few ingredients or equipment. By the time he returned home Paul was hooked, and knew he wanted to work in the world of catering.

Paul attended Plymouth catering college where he discovered a natural flair for cooking and as part of his course he spent time in the Jura Mountains in France. Paul loved France so much that he stayed there for three years, learning about Mediterranean cooking. However, Paul wanted to experience other areas of the catering industry and has worked as a waiter at the House of Commons (in fact he was working there the night that Mrs Thatcher was deposed); at various catering outlets on animal safari parks and a chain of bakery stores.

When satellite TV was launched Paul was headhunted for a position in television food styling and worked for a

top to bottom:
"urgh! Too much salt!"
"Busy creating..."
"Who's for tea?"

lot of top chefs, preparing dishes for "Here's One I Made Earlier". Paul has worked for all the major shopping channels and does cooking demonstrations around the UK and Ireland. Paul is now considered the most respected and popular guest presenter on one of the country's top shopping channels, and that's where I met him.

I've a true passion for food and describe myself as an enthusiastic amateur. My background in catering started in the 70's with the hotel industry and since then I've attended several courses with top cooks and chefs, to keep me up to date with what's fresh and new. My children, Darren and Hayley, have grown up and left home now and I live with my husband Steve with our two cats, Delia and Carrot, close to the Norfolk border. You may recognise me from modelling various products on shopping television. Like Paul, I truly believe that cooking doesn't have to be a chore.

We want you to read this book as you would a magazine, to find out what is on the telly. Keep the book next to you and use it to give you inspiration and time saving advice. As you explore the following pages, you'll find Top Tips and advice to help you create what you want, with (mostly) everyday ingredients. And you'll find out more about Paul and me, which will hopefully bring a smile!

Please let us have your comments and feedback about the recipes and maybe you have favourite recipes that you'd also like to share? Just let us know and you could be featured in our next book!

Dee and parents meeting the captain on board
cruise ship Arkadia a "couple" of years ago!

So, whether you're a novice or a more experienced cook, you'll find all your needs are catered for here.

Enjoy!

Paul Brodel. PO Box 1, Harston, Cambridge. CB22 7PX

cook@paulbrodel.co.uk

www.paulbrodel.co.uk

Top Tip:

"You can freeze this soup. Make the recipe as far as number 8 and then freeze it. When you reheat it, just add the cream and parsley when you are ready to serve"

Potato and Onion Soup

Ingredients

3 large baking potatoes

3 medium onions (chopped)

25g (1 oz) butter

570ml (1pt) chicken or vegetable stock
(ready-made or made with 2 stock cubes)

1 small pot double cream

2 tbsp sweet sherry

1 tsp dried or fresh chopped parsley

1 fat clove garlic (crushed)

Salt and pepper to taste

25g (1 oz) grated mature cheddar cheese *(optional)*

1 packet croutons *(optional)*

Method

1. In the butter, gently fry the onion with the garlic for five minutes, until soft and clear

2. Peel and cube the potatoes (approx. 2cm or ½" cubes)

3. Add the potatoes to the onions and garlic and cook together for another three minutes so the potatoes take on their flavours

4. Add the stock

5. Bring to the boil

6. Add the sherry

7. Simmer for about twenty minutes until the potatoes are tender

8. Blend together with a hand blender, stick blender or food processor

9. Return to the saucepan on a low heat. Do not boil. Then stir in the cream and the parsley, and season to taste.

10. Serve with croutons and grated, mature cheddar cheese sprinkled on top. So delicious!

Top Tip:

"If you find the butternut squash too hard to chop, then place in a microwave for 4 minutes on full power to help to soften it"

Butternut Squash Soup

Ingredients

1 medium sized butternut squash.
2 medium sized onions finely chopped
570ml (1 pt) milk
275ml (½ pt) chicken or vegetable stock
50g (2 oz) butter
1tsp granulated sugar
1 medium potato
Salt and pepper to taste
Chopped chives and Parmesan shavings to garnish

Method

1. Peel, de-seed and chop the butternut squash into approx. 2 cm (1/2") cubes.

2. Peel and chop the potato into similar sized cubes.

3. Place the butternut squash, potatoes, chopped onions, sugar, butter and stock into a microwaveable bowl. Cover with clingfilm and pierce the top. Cook in the microwave for 20 minutes on full power.

4. Create a hole in the centre of the cling film and pour in the milk. Use a stick blender to blend until smooth, leaving the clingfilm on so as not to make a mess everywhere! Reheat on full power for a further 5 minutes.

5. Season to taste.

6. Garnish with chives and Parmesan shavings and, to make it extra rich, add a swirl of cream.

Variations

This recipe can be used for most vegetables soups. Just change the butternut squash for some of the following:
Carrots, broccoli, parsnips, red peppers, sweet potatoes, cauliflower or any combination of them.
Your imagination is the only limitation and it is so easy to do!

Top Tip:

"Serve as a snack or starter on shredded lettuce, with a segment of lemon, mango chutney and yoghurt. If you like it hotter put two tablespoons of chilli sauce in the mixture"

Onion Bhajis

Ingredients

110g (4 oz) plain flour
175g (6oz) finely sliced onions
150g (6oz) finely shredded carrots
Salt and pepper to taste
½ tsp paprika
1 tbsp fresh, chopped, coriander leaves
½ tsp granulated sugar
Juice of ¼ lemon
Vegetable oil for frying

Method

1. In a large mixing bowl, mix together the flour, onions, carrots, paprika, coriander, sugar, lemon juice and salt and pepper. Add a little water and stir, to form the mixture into a dough.

2. Shape the mixture into balls about the size of a large marble

3. Place a few of the bhajis in to the basket of a fryer heated to180°C and fry until golden brown (about 6 to 8 minutes).

4. Place on kitchen towel to drain off any excess oil.

Top Tip:
   "Serve with mixed salad leaves and garlic mayonnaise. You can also make these with cream cheese instead of pate, as a great vegetarian starter. If you're making your own breadcrumbs in a food processor, you can always make extra and freeze them for another time"

Stuffed Mushrooms

Ingredients

225g (8 oz) medium sized mushrooms
50g (2 oz) liver pate
1 egg
110g (4 oz) breadcrumbs
110g (4 oz) plain flour
½ tsp of mixed herbs

Method

1. Wipe the mushrooms with kitchen paper and remove the stalks.

2. Fill the mushrooms with pate.

3. Place the flour in one bowl, whisk up the egg in another and place the breadcrumbs and mixed herbs together in a third.

4. Dip the mushrooms in the flour, then the egg and finally the breadcrumbs.

5. Place the mushrooms into a fryer at 180°C for about 3 minutes until golden brown.

6. Drain the cooked mushrooms on a paper towel.

Top Tip:

"Serve with salad and sweet chilli sauce dip. The toasts may be made in advance and kept in the freezer, provided your prawns are fresh and have not already been frozen"

Sesame Prawn Toast

Ingredients

10 slices thinly sliced white bread (crusts removed)

3 tbsp white sesame seeds

450g (1lb) raw peeled prawns

1 egg

1tbsp chopped spring onions

1 tsp peeled, fresh ginger

1tbsp light soy sauce

½ tsp sesame oil

1 tbsp sweet chilli sauce (optional)

Vegetable or sunflower oil for deep frying

Method

1. Place the prawns, spring onions, ginger, chilli sauce, soy sauce, sesame oil and egg into a food processor and mix up to a paste.

2. Spread the prawn paste over the bread, like a thick layer of butter.

3. Dip the prawn paste side into the sesame seeds and then cut each slice into 4 triangles.

4. Deep fry for about three minutes in hot oil (about 180°C) until golden brown.

Top Tip:

"If you want to glaze with egg, this gives a lovely shine to the rolls. Also, once at step 6, you can add flavourings such as mixed herbs, marinades, cheese, sun-dried tomatoes, ham, fried onions or seeds. With a sweet flavoured bread, like raisin and sultana, I like to mix a little saffron in with the milk to give a wonderful yellow colour to the rolls"

Bread Rolls

Ingredients
225g (8 oz) strong, plain flour or bread flour
½ tsp salt
1 tsp caster sugar
25g (1 oz) butter (melted)
150mls (¼ pt) warm milk
13g (½ oz) fresh yeast

Method

1. Mix the yeast with the luke warm milk and sugar.

2. Leave for five minutes.

3. Place the flour and salt into a bowl and mix in the melted butter.

4. Add the yeast liquid and mix to a soft dough.

5. Knead for ten minutes, until the dough becomes firm and elastic.

6. Place the dough into a bowl and cover with a clean, damp cloth. Leave in a warm place for ten minutes.

7. Knead the dough again for two minutes, to reduce it to its original size.

8. Then divide into about 6 to 8 rolls.

9. Bake at gas mark 7 or 220°C for about 15 to 20 minutes or until golden brown.

Top Tip:

"Serve as a starter with lemon wedges, rocket salad and toast. Or, stir the remaining prawns into the mixture and serve in little bowls topped with smoked salmon"

Easy Prawn Mousse

Ingredients

275g (10 oz) ready cooked prawns

110g (4 oz) Greek yoghurt

150g (5 oz) cream cheese with herbs

Juice ½ lemon

Juice ½ lime

1 tbsp fresh, chopped dill

1 tbsp fresh, chopped chives

Salt and black pepper

Method

1. Place 200g (7 oz) of the prawns into a food processor and mix to a paste.

2. Add the Greek yoghurt and cream cheese and mix again.

3. Then add the herbs, lemon and lime juice. Mix once more and season to taste.

4. Garnish with the remaining prawns.

Top Tip:

"Humous can be served as a dip with sliced, raw vegetables or as a starter with toasted pita bread and lemon. Dust the humous with a pinch of paprika. If you're using the sesame seeds instead of tahini, it is really important to toast them first, as this helps to really bring out the flavour. Simply place them in a frying pan on a medium-high heat, stirring continuously until they are a nice golden brown, then place on a cold plate to cool"

Parma Ham and Humous Rolls

Ingredients

8 slices Parma ham

For the Humous:-

1 tin chickpeas (drained) or 250g (10 oz) cooked chickpeas

3 cloves garlic

5 tbsp olive oil

Juice 1 lemon

2 tbsp Tahini paste or 4 tbsp toasted sesame seeds

2 tbsp mayonnaise (optional)

¼ tsp sugar

Salt and black pepper

Pinch of paprika

Method

1. Place all the humous ingredients into a food processor and mix to a fine paste. Season to taste.

2. Lay a slice of Parma ham on a chopping board and spread a layer of humous on it and wrap up into a roll. Repeat until all the slices of ham are filled and chill in the fridge.

3. Slice into wheels and serve as a starter or canapé.

Top Tip:
   "To make garlic mayonnaise, add two cloves of garlic to the mixture. Alternatively, you could add mixed herbs, black pepper, chilli sauce, mango chutney or mint jelly to the basic mayonnaise for a host of variations. If you want a richer mayonnaise, add an extra egg yolk. This is also a good idea if, at your first attempt, the mixture curdles. Simply add the extra egg yolk to the bottom of the container, pour the mixture on top and start to blend again"

Mayonnaise

Ingredients
1 egg
1tsp Dijon mustard
1tsp lemon juice
Salt and pepper
275ml (10 fl oz) groundnut or sunflower oil

Method

1. Place the egg, mustard, lemon juice and salt and pepper into a stick blender beaker or strong pint glass.

2. Tilt the beaker or glass to the side and slowly pour in the oil, so it floats above the egg.

3. Place your stick blender slowly into all the ingredients so as not to mix them up.

4. Once the base of the stick blender is at the bottom of the beaker on top of the egg, turn on power and mix. Do not move the stick blender until you see the mayonnaise forming, then slowly move it from side to side to mix in the rest of the oil and then move it upwards.

Top Tip:

"For traditional Marie Rose Sauce, leave out the brandy. The sauce is delicious served with soft avocado accompanied by our warm bread rolls"

Prawn Cocktail with Cognac Sauce

Ingredients

500g (18 oz) cooked prawns

250g (9 oz) cooked tiger prawns

Sauce: -

6 tbsp mayonnaise

4 tbsp tomato sauce

2 tbsp double cream

Salt and black pepper

1 tsp lemon juice

2 tsp brandy

Splash Worcestershire Sauce

To garnish: -

Iceberg lettuce or any mixed salad leaves

Tomato

Lemon

Fresh parsley

Cayenne pepper

Method

1. Shred the iceberg lettuce and place in Paris goblets or any other serving dishes you choose.

2. Divide the cooked prawns equally between the goblets, and then add the tiger prawns saving some for garnish.

3. Make the sauce by mixing all sauce ingredients together and stirring well.

4. Drizzle the sauce over the prawns.

5. Garnish with the saved tiger prawns and wedges of lemon and tomato. Add a sprig of parsley and dust with cayenne pepper.

Top Tip:

"This makes a tasty and light starter, however if you'd like it for a more substantial lunch dish, just add Parma ham and fresh figs and serve with some crusty bread. Irresistible! I find the best balsamic vinegars are the ones that say they are a glaze, available in most supermarkets. Years ago, I had to make my own glaze by adding a tablespoon of brown sugar to a bottle of balsamic vinegar, then reducing it over the stove and until it was a third of its original volume. This makes it really thick and sweeter and brings out so much flavour. Well worth it!"

Mozzarella and Tomato Salad with Balsamic Dressing

Ingredients

2 packs soft mozzarella cheese
3 large ripe beef tomatoes
A good handful fresh basil leaves
4 tsp balsamic vinegar
6 tsp extra virgin olive oil
Salt and ground black pepper

Method

1. Open and drain the cheese, and slice each into six.

2. Wash and dry the tomatoes and slice into six rounds each.

3. Make the dressing by whisking the oil and vinegar together, then adding salt and pepper to taste.

4. Arrange the cheese and tomatoes on serving plates and drizzle with the dressing.

5. Finish by scattering the basil leaves and grinding a little more black pepper over each dish.

Top Tip:

"This dish is a very tasty starter for around 6 people, however it can be served as a vegetarian main course with sweet potato mash and crusty bread. You can also change the cous cous for cooked rice and make it heartier by adding fried minced beef, lamb or lean turkey (healthy option) with onions. This makes it really tasty."

Stuffed Peppers and Tomatoes

Ingredients

1 bag of 3 mixed peppers
3 large ripe beef tomatoes
2 packs cous cous (of your choice)
50g (2 oz) Parmesan cheese
50g (2 oz) strong cheddar cheese
75g (3 oz) fresh white breadcrumbs
1 tbsp olive oil
Freshly ground black pepper

Method

1. Pre heat oven to 180°C or gas mark 4.

2. Slice the peppers in half and remove all the seeds and do the same with the tomatoes.

3. Place the peppers and tomatoes in an ovenproof dish. Drizzle with olive oil and sprinkle with pepper. Place in the oven for 10 minutes.

4. Make up the cous cous as directed on the pack.

5. Finely grate both cheeses.

6. Remove the peppers and tomatoes from the oven and fill each one with the cous cous.

7. In a bowl, mix the cheeses and breadcrumbs together and top each pepper and tomato with this mixture.

8. Turn the oven up to 220°C or gas mark 7 and bake for a further 15 minutes, until the cheese has melted and the topping is a light golden brown.

Top Tip:

"You can use these special hot dogs to serve with pre-dinner drinks, at BBQ's or as a tasty treat at a children's party. You can also add some fried onions to the bread mix when you add the corn, yum! These can also be cooked in the omelette maker "

Special Hot Dogs

Ingredients
1 pack good frankfurters
1 small tin creamed sweet corn
1 500g pack white bread mix

Method

1. Make up the bread mix as directed on the pack.

2. At the last kneading stage, add the tin of creamed corn a tablespoonful at a time and check to make sure the mixture isn't too wet. If it does become too wet add a little self-raising flour.

3. When the bread is ready to cook, roll out the dough and cut into squares for the number of frankfurters you have.

4. Place one frankfurter in each square of dough and simply roll up so the frankfurter sticks out at each end.

5. Bake as directed on the bread pack and serve warm.

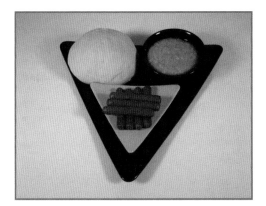

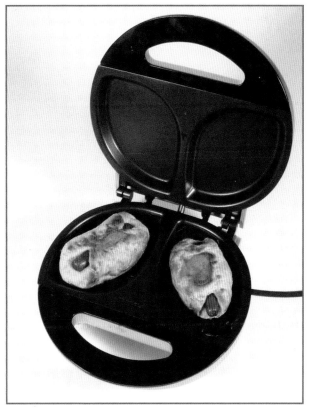

Top Tip:

"If you do not like crab don't worry, you can use raw prawns instead. Just make sure they are finely chopped. You can pre-prepare the mix a day in advance as long as its kept really chilled. A real time saver! If you want to make Thai crab cakes, simply add red Thai "Shake It Ups" to the ingredients"

Crab Cakes

Ingredients

1 tin white crab meat

1 egg

1 tsp mayonnaise

275g (10 oz) fresh white breadcrumbs

2 chopped spring onions

1 tsp dried dill

200g (7 oz) self-raising flour

Salt and freshly ground black pepper

Vegetable or sunflower oil for shallow frying

Method

1. Open and drain the crab meat and place in large bowl.

2. Separate the egg. Put the yolk to one side and whisk the white until it's just fluffy not stiff.

3. Finely chop the spring onions.

4. Break up the crab meat gently with a fork. You don't want to end up with a paste.

5. Add the mayonnaise, breadcrumbs, spring onions and dill to the crab meat and stir.

6. Next, gently stir in the egg white. At this stage the mixture should be soft but not sloppy. If you find it is too sloppy, just add more breadcrumbs.

7. Add a little water to the egg yolk and whisk.

8. Place the flour on a shallow plate season with salt and pepper.

9. Take a tablespoon of the crab mixture and mould into a small cake shape. Dip it gently in the egg then finely coat with the flour. This mixture should make approximately 10 cakes.

10. Heat the oil in a large frying pan to a medium heat.

11. Fry the cakes for a minute on each side or until they are a light golden brown colour. Serve warm, with little gem lettuce, mayonnaise and lime wedges.

"These little balls make such a tasty warm or cold starter served on a bed of lettuce with lemon wedges. They can be made two days in advance and stored in the fridge. If you want to make a main meal with them, just make larger balls and serve hot with home made chips, a pickled cucumber and tomato ketchup"

This was one of Dee's mum's favourites and went down well when she entertained. It's served in memory of her, on her special dinner set

Celia's Jewish Salmon Balls

Ingredients

1 240g tin red salmon
1 large mild onion
1 large egg
150g (5 oz) Matzo meal (medium or fine)
Salt and pepper
Sunflower oil for deep-frying

Method

1. Open and drain the salmon removing any bones.

2. Peel and chop the onion in half and place in a food processor. Pulse until the onion becomes a paste.

3. Add the salmon to the onion and pulse until blended.

4. Add the egg and mix for 20 seconds.

5. Then add the Matzo meal and pulse until the mixture is firm enough to shape. If the mixture is too wet, just add a little more Matzo meal and if it's too dry just add one more egg. Add salt and pepper to taste.

6. Heat up the fryer to 180°C.

7. Mould the mixture into balls the size of a two-pound coin. This amount should make between 20 to 25 balls.

8. Fry for 2 minutes or until the balls are a dark golden brown colour.

9. Drain on kitchen paper.

Top Tip:
   "You can make herb dumplings by adding a few mixed herbs or some of the garlic and herb marinade from the "Shake it Up" range, as you mix the flour and suet together"

Beef Stew and Dumplings

Ingredients
Serves 4
Stew: -
500g (18 oz) stewing steak (cubed)
1 chopped medium sized onion
2 large carrots (chopped)
1 small turnip (chopped)
3 peeled and diced potatoes
2 meat Oxo stock cubes
1 ½ ltr water
2 tbsp plain flour
1 tbsp soy sauce (optional)
2 oz butter or margarine
2 rashers streaky bacon cut bitesize

Ingredients
Serves 4
Dumplings: -
225g (8 oz) self-raising flour
110g (4 oz) suet
Water

Method

1. Using the butter or margarine, fry the bacon and beef in a pan.

2. Add the plain flour and mix.

3. Then add the stock cubes, water and the chopped vegetables.

4. Bring to the boil and add the soy sauce.

Method

1. Mix the flour and suet together with a little water to form a stiff dough, then roll out into balls.

2. Cook in the simmering stew for the last twenty minutes of its cooking time.

4. Cover with a lid and simmer for 1 ½ hours, adding more water if needed, then season to taste.

5. Add the dumplings 20 minutes before the stew is ready to serve.

Top Tip:

"Battered king prawns are great served with sweet chilli sauce and salad as a starter. Use this batter on some nice cod for a fish and chip supper, or with chicken or pork and rice with sweet and sour sauce as a main course. With chicken or pork, use rice flour to coat the meat, instead of normal flour, before dipping in the batter and frying"

Beer Batter for Prawns, Pork, Chicken, Fish and Vegetables

Ingredients

110g (4 oz) plain flour
¼ tsp salt
1 egg
75ml (3 fl oz) milk
75 ml (3 fl oz) beer
¼ tsp turmeric to give a nice colour (optional)

Method

1. Place all the above ingredients into a food processor and blend until a smooth batter is formed. You can also do this with a hand whisk.

2. The batter is best if left to stand, covered, for about two hours but it's not the end of the world if you don't have time.

3. Flour your chosen food, then dip the pieces in batter and shake off any excess.

4. Deep fry at 180°C until cooked.

Top Tip:

"This dish can be placed under a grill to brown the top if you wish. Also, before you add the cream, you can add a selection of vegetables to turn the dish into a creamy vegetable bake. An ideal vegetarian main course. The "Shake it Up" garlic and herb marinade is a great addition too, to really boost the flavour or if you don't have fresh garlic"

Potato Gratin with Sweet Potato

Ingredients

700g (1 ½ lb) peeled and thinly sliced potatoes
350g (12 oz) peeled and thinly sliced sweet potatoes
2 medium onions (chopped)
300mls (11 fl oz) of double cream
3 cloves of garlic (crushed)
50g (2 oz) of butter
50g (2 oz) of grated cheddar cheese

Method

1. Place the onions and potatoes into a large frying pan with the butter and fry without browning for about 10 minutes.

2. Add the sweet potatoes and fry for a further 15 minutes, on a medium heat.

3. Next add the garlic and stir fry for two minutes.

4. Add the double cream and cook for a further ten minutes, or until the potatoes are fully cooked.

5. Finish off with the grated cheese on top.

Top Tip:
    "The reason for not using olive oil is that it burns at a much lower temperature, and I also leave the garlic to the last couple of minutes of cooking time as it too can burn if added early and gives a bitter flavour"

Top Tip:
    "This is so good with duck, game or Dee's Gammon with Sherry, served with mashed potato. Delicious! And it's virtually fat free!"

Stir Fry Cabbage with Ginger and Garlic
and
Red Cabbage with Cranberry and Redcurrant Jelly

<table>
<tr><td>

Ingredients
½ a Savoy cabbage (shredded)
2 cloves of finely chopped garlic
2 tsp of vegetable oil (not olive oil)
15g (½ oz) butter
1 ½ cm cube fresh ginger (finely chopped)
1 tsp dark soy sauce

</td><td>

Ingredients
1 red cabbage (shredded)
2 tbsp cranberry sauce
2tbsp redcurrant jelly
2 tbsp sultanas (optional)

</td></tr>
</table>

Method

1. Place the oil and butter in pan and heat.

2. Add the cabbage and fry until it begins to soften.

3. Then add the ginger and garlic and fry for a further 3 minutes.

4. Finally add the soy sauce. Stir and cook for one minute, then serve.

Method

1. Place the shredded cabbage in a microwave dish and add the cranberry sauce, redcurrant jelly and sultanas.

2. Cover and cook on full power for 10 minutes. Stir and then leave to rest for 10 minutes.

3. Cook for a further 5 minutes on full power, then serve.

    OR fry in wok for 10 mins

Top Tip:
"Serve with rice or cous cous and a tomato and onion salad. This dish tastes so delicious once the paprika has been allowed to infuse with all the different ingredients"

Chicken Paprika

Ingredients
6 chicken thighs
1 tbsp oil
1 large onion (chopped)
2 tbsp nice red paprika (the duller it is the older it is)
2 tins chopped tomatoes in juice
1 chicken stock cube dissolved in 570ml (1 pt) boiling water
1 red pepper (sliced)
75g (3 oz) chestnut mushrooms (sliced)
3 tbsp tomato puree
1 tbsp plain flour
Salt and pepper

Method

1. Place the chicken and onions in a large pan with a little oil and fry until the chicken pieces begin to brown.

2. Add the paprika and sliced red pepper.

3. Fry for another five minutes, then add the flour and stir thouroughly.

4. Next add the tins of tomatoes, tomato puree, stock, mushrooms and season with the salt and pepper.

5. Bring to the boil and simmer on a low heat for 45 minutes, or cook in the oven at 180°C or gas mark 4.

Top Tip:
   "You can cook this on the stove by adding a little oil to the rice first and frying for two minutes, then add the rest of the ingredients, bring to the boil and simmer for 15 minutes. This is how you make authentic pilaf rice...you decide! If you want to cook this for more than one person just multiply all the ingredients accordingly"

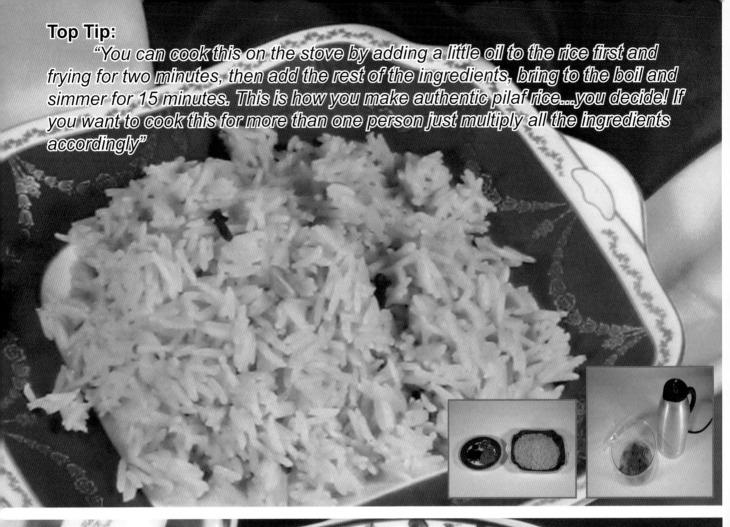

Top Tip:
 "You must make sure the sesame seed oil is just smoking as this releases loads of flavour, but you must not leave this unattended.
If you want to create special fried rice, there are loads of extra things you can add to make a wonderful meal in itself. Why not try some of these options..."

Spring onions
Fried onions
Ham
Cooked prawns
Peas
Cooked pork or chicken
Fried peppers
Fried mushrooms (chestnut ones have loads of flavour)
Fried scallops
Fried cooked and sliced crispy duck with hoisin sauce
Pineapple with cashew nuts

Pilaf Rice & Egg Fried Rice

Pilaf Rice (The Cheating Version!)
Ingredients
1 cup (about 150g) Basmati rice per person (large portion)
1 cardamom pod
2 cloves
3 saffron strands (optional)
¼ tsp turmeric
2 cups boiling water

Method

1. Place all the dry ingredients together in a microwave dish.
2. Add the boiling water and stir.
3. Immediately cover the dish and put it into the microwave on medium power for 15 minutes.
4. Stir again and then rest for five minutes.

Ingredients
Egg Fried Rice
4 cups of the plain cooked rice (as above)
1 egg, lightly beaten
½ tsp sesame seed oil
1 tsp dark soy sauce

Method

1. Place the sesame seed oil in a hot wok until it just starts to smoke. Be careful this is very hot!
2. Add the cooked rice and start to stir.
3. Next add the soy sauce and keep stirring.
4. Once the rice is thoroughly hot, make a well in the centre and add the egg. If you want very fine strands of egg, stir and mix immediately. If you prefer larger pieces of egg, allow the egg to set slightly, before stirring and then serve.

Ingredients
Plain Rice
1 cup (about 150g) American long grain <u>parboiled</u> rice
2 cups boiling water.

Method

It needs to be parboiled to stop it sticking together, just make sure you get the right one. I made it with just American long grain once and ended up with a sticky mess!

In the MICROWAVE:

1. Place 1 cup of rice to 2 cups of boiling water into a microwave dish and cook in the microwave on medium heat for 15 mins.
2. Allow to stand for 5 minutes. Perfect!

On the HOB:

1. Place the rice and boiling water in a pan.
2. Bring to the boil and then simmer on the lowest heat for 15minutes with the lid on.
3. Stir occasionally, and then at the end of the cooking time, allow to stand for 5 minutes.

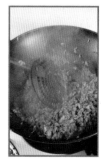

Top Tip:

"Place some cheese and breadcrumbs over the top of the mash before baking, to make a lovely thick crust. Try changing the topping by adding parsnips or turnip, or just have it with plain mashed potato. You can vary the filling to a curried mince, by adding two tablespoons of curry powder to the meat when frying. Delicious! To reduce the fat in the mince, fry it separately first, then place it in a sieve and pour over boiling water. Add the mince back to the pan and continue. It really doesn't take away the flavour"

Cottage Pie with Sweet Potato

Ingredients

450g (1 lb) fresh minced beef
2 onions (chopped)
2 tbsp plain flour
2 beef Oxo stock cubes and
500ml (17 fl oz) water (for stock)
2 medium carrots (chopped)
1 tsp Worcestershire Sauce (optional)
1tsp soy sauce (optional)
½ tsp mixed herbs (optional)
50g (2 oz) frozen peas (optional)
Topping:
800g (1¾ lbs) potatoes
400g (14 oz) sweet potatoes
50g (2 oz) butter
A little milk
Salt and pepper

Method

Topping:

1. Peel the potatoes and sweet potatoes and cut into even sized pieces.
2. Place in a pan and cover with water add pinch of salt
3. Bring to boil and simmer for 20 minutes.

Filling:

1. Place the onions and minced beef in a medium hot pan and fry gently until the meat has browned.
2. Stir in the flour, then add the stock slowly, stirring all the time. At this stage, also add any of the optional ingredients you choose.
3. Bring to the boil and simmer for 10 minutes.
4. Place the meat mixture in an ovenproof dish.
5. Mash the boiled potatoes and add the butter, milk and seasoning.
6. Place the mash on top of the mince and smooth over the surface with a fork.
7. Bake in the oven at 200°C/gas mark 6, for 20 to 30 minutes until the mash is golden brown.

Top Tip:

"You'll love this with homemade mash and steamed vegetables. So nice to come home to after a walk on a winter's day! If you would like it extra orangey, take away ½ tbsp brown sugar and add 1 tbsp of marmalade. If you want the "poor man's" version, fry up some sausages and lightly toast some bread, then spread the bread with marmalade and roll the sausage inside. Not to everyone's taste, but I think it's lovely. Please don't think I'm mad!"

Pork Chops in Orange Sauce

Ingredients

4 pork chops
2 ½ tbsp flour
1 tbsp of oil
2 oranges (peeled sliced and de-seeded)
2 tbsp brown sugar
250mls (9 fl oz) orange juice
250mls (9 fl oz) boiling water
1 chicken stock cube
½ tsp of mixed herbs
1 large onion (finely chopped)
Salt and pepper

Method

1. Season the flour with salt and pepper and place on a plate. Coat the chops in the flour.

2. Fry the chops in half the oil and seal on both sides until lightly browned.

3. Add the rest of the oil, then the chopped onions and fry for three minutes.

4. Add the remaining flour and stir well.

5. Mix the orange juice, water and stock cube and slowly add to chops.

6. Next add the herbs, sugar and orange slices.

7. Bring to the boil and simmer, covered for 45 minutes to 1 hour, until the chops are tender. Add a little more water if the sauce is too thick. If it is a little too thin, leave the lid off for the last ten minutes of cooking time to allow the sauce to thicken.

8. Instead of simmering on the stove, you can place the chops in an oven dish and cook in the oven at gas mark 4 /180°C for 1 hour leaving the lid off for the last 10 minutes.

Top Tip:

"This is a fantastic sauce and so easy to make. I usually make a large batch and freeze it in portions. Also it is very versatile. You can add peas and carrots and turn it into a savoury mince with dumplings, or add one of Paul's sauces and turn it into chilli or even sweet and sour mince with rice. Try the chilli mince to fill tacos and serve with a green salad. You could also use this sauce as a thick pizza topping. Delicious!"

Bolognese Sauce

Ingredients

175g (6 oz) minced beef
3 rashers smoked bacon (cut bitesize)
4 large mushrooms (sliced)
1 large onion (chopped)
2 cloves garlic (crushed)
1 400g tin chopped tomatoes
1 tbsp tomato puree
2 tbsp tomato ketchup
6 fresh basil leaves (chopped)
A glass of red wine
Salt and pepper to taste
2 tbsp of olive oil

Method

1. In a large pan, gently fry the onions until soft.

2. Add the bacon, mushrooms and garlic and fry for a further 4 minutes.

3. Turn the heat to medium and add the minced beef. Stir until the mince is brown.

4. Now turn the heat to its highest setting and add the wine, tomato ketchup, tomato puree and tin of tomatoes.

5. Stir for one minute then turn the heat down to a very low simmer.

6. Add the basil leaves and salt and pepper.

7. Leave to simmer for 1 hour. You need this sauce to be very concentrated to allow all the wonderful flavours to infuse together.

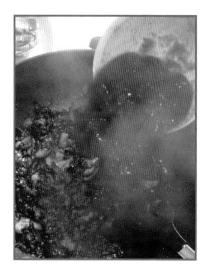

Top Tip:

"Coat chicken pieces in rice flour, then dip into a mixture of cornflour and water, using it as a light batter, and fry in hot oil. Add this to the sauce for a delicious sweet and sour chicken, Hong Kong style. The same can be done with prawns. My favourite!"

Sweet and Sour Sauce

Ingredients

110g (4 oz) granulated or caster sugar
4 tbsp malt vinegar
2 tbsp light soy sauce
1 ½ tbsp cornflour
1 red pepper (diced)
250ml (9 fl oz) tomato ketchup
                 (economy label is fine)
1 onion (cut into chunky pieces)
2 tbsp mango chutney
1 small tin pineapple pieces in juice
200ml (7 fl oz) boiling water
A little oil for frying

Method

1. Fry the peppers and onions for five minute in a frying pan.

2. Add the sugar, vinegar, soy sauce, tomato ketchup, mango chutney and pineapple pieces with the juice and water, and bring to the boil for five mins.

3. Blend the cornflour with a little water and add to the sauce, stirring all the time.

4. Simmer for a further 10 minutes.

You can vary the amount of sugar you use to taste, depending on how sweet or sour you like the sauce.

Top Tip:

"Fry some cubed chicken fillets, add the sauce and simmer for 15 minutes for a delicious chicken curry. Serve with rice. Also good with tiger prawns"

Curry Sauce

Ingredients

1 onion (finely chopped)
1 clove garlic (crushed)
1 cooking apple (peeled cored and chopped)
250ml (9 fl oz) chicken stock (made with 1 stock cube)
25g (1 oz) sultanas
50g (2 oz) curry powder
1 tbsp flour
25g (1 oz) butter or oil
1tbsp mango chutney
½ tsp soy sauce
25g (1 oz) chopped, dried apricots (optional)
1tsp of sweet chilli sauce (optional)

Method

1. Fry the chopped onion and apple with the curry powder in the butter or oil, for about 5 minutes on a medium heat.

2. Add the crushed garlic and fry for a further minute.

3. Stir in the flour and cook for thirty seconds

4. Slowly add the chicken stock, stirring all the time and gradually bring to the boil.

5. Continue to stir as you add the mango chutney, soy sauce, sweet chilli sauce, sultanas and apricots.

6. Simmer, covered, for 15 minutes on a low heat.

Top Tip:
     "Great with pasta or as a rich pizza topping.
     Also delicious at a BBQ with sausages or burgers"

Rich Bacon and Tomato Sauce

Ingredients

1 x 425g (15oz) tin chopped tomatoes in juice
1 onion (chopped)
2 rashers bacon (chopped)
¼ tsp dried or fresh mixed herbs
¼ tsp soy sauce
50g (2oz) sliced mushrooms (chestnut mushrooms have the most flavour)
12g (½ oz) plain flour
12g (½ oz) butter

Method

1. Fry the chopped onions and bacon in the butter for about 5 minutes.

2. Stir in the flour, cook for 30 seconds.

3. Gradually add the tomatoes, soy sauce, herbs and mushrooms stirring constantly.

4. Bring to the boil, then simmer for 10 minutes. Add a little water if the sauce becomes too thick.

5. Season to taste.

Top Tip:

"Great hot or cold served at a picnic or sliced up at a buffet. Dee fell in love with this. So tasty!"

Some different toppings: -
Pepperoni
Ham
Sliced peppers
Spicy mince
Olives
Different cheeses
Anchovies
Mushrooms
Fried leeks
Parma ham
Artichokes
Egg

Scone Pizza

Ingredients

For the Scones

225g (8oz) self raising flour

50g (2 oz) margarine or olive oil

50g (2 oz) grated cheddar cheese

125mls (4 fl oz) milk

Salt

For the Topping

4 tbsp of tomato ketchup

1 onion (chopped)

50g (2 oz) grated cheddar cheese

3 rashers bacon (sliced)

2 tomatoes (sliced)

Mixed herbs

Method

1. Make the scone dough by placing the margarine or olive oil and flour into a food processor and mix until it looks like fine breadcrumbs.

2. Add the cheese and a little of the milk.

3. Mix, adding the remainder of the milk a little at a time until it forms a dough.

4. Roll out to form a circle about ½ cm thick.

5. Place the tomato ketchup on top and add the onion, bacon, sliced tomatoes and finish off with the grated cheese.

6. Sprinkle with a pinch of mixed herbs.

7. Place in hot oven at 220°C / gas mark 7, for 15 to 20 minutes until cooked and well risen.

Top Tip:

"So nice on a picnic, or for a summer dinner with potato salad and mixed leaves. Once you have tried homemade Scotch egg, you'll never want to buy ready made ones again!"

Scotch Eggs

Ingredients

5 eggs
300g (11 oz) pork sausage meat
250g (9 oz) breadcrumbs
110g (4 oz) plain flour

Method

1. Boil 4 of the eggs for about 10 minutes until hard-boiled.

2. Cool them in cold water and remove the shells.

3. Place the flour in one bowl, the remaining egg (lightly beaten), in another and the breadcrumbs in a third bowl.

4. Divide the sausage meat into four.

5. Mould the sausage meat around each hard-boiled egg. (If you dip your hands in the flour first, it will stop the sausage meat sticking to your fingers!)

6. Roll each sausage meat covered egg in flour, then in the beaten egg and lastly in the breadcrumbs.

7. You can deep fry at 170°C or shallow fry in a little oil, turning frequently until cooked and golden brown.

Top Tip:
    "Pesto is quite a personal thing, so none of this is set in stone! You can add anchovies to the mixture if you choose. You can also swap the basil leaves for roasted red peppers and some sun-dried tomatoes to make red pepper pesto. This is great to mix with pasta or as a topping for fish or chicken. Our favourite way to serve this dish is with baby carrots, peas and new potatoes tossed in butter and mint. If you want to try something different just exchange the green pesto for red pesto, it's up to you"

Salmon Fillets with Crunchy Pesto Topping

Ingredients

For the Pesto

2 large handfuls of basil leaves

4 tbsp of extra virgin olive oil

50g (2 oz) Parmesan cheese

50g (2 oz) pine nuts

2 peeled cloves garlic

Salt and pepper to taste

For the Main Dish

4 Salmon fillets

1 Jar of ready-made pesto or Paul's homemade pesto

75g (3 oz) grated Parmesan cheese

50g (2 oz) fresh, white breadcrumbs

1 lemon

1 lime

Freshly ground black pepper

Method

Pesto

1. Place all the ingredients into a food processor and mix until a wonderful, smooth green paste is achieved.

Main Dish

1. Pre heat the oven to 180°C/gas mark 4.

2. Wash and dry the salmon fillets and place in an ovenproof dish.

3. Zest and juice the lemon and lime.

4. Spread the top of each salmon fillet with about two teaspoons of pesto.

5. Mix the juice from the lemon and lime together and pour over the salmon and pesto.

6. Mix the breadcrumbs, parmesan, lemon and lime zest and pepper together and sprinkle over each salmon fillet.

7. Place in the oven cook for 10 minutes, then turn oven up to 225°C/gas mark 6 and cook for a further 10 to15 minutes until the topping is a golden brown colour.

Top Tip:

*"Don't worry if the cheese spills out while it's cooking.
It gets nice and gooey, so make sure you serve it! I have found boursin
cheam cheese is the best to use, however you can use what you like. If
you haven't got Parma ham try smoked streaky bacon instead"*

Stuffed Chicken Breasts

Ingredients

4 chicken breasts
1 pack Boursin cream cheese with herb and garlic
4 slices Parma ham
1 lemon
Fresh parsley

Method

1. Pre heat the oven to 200°C/gas mark 6.

2. Wash and dry the chicken breasts.

3. Cut a slit, lengthways in each chicken breast and fill with the cheese.

4. Wrap a slice of Parma ham around each chicken breast.

5. Place all the chicken breasts in a lightly oiled, ovenproof dish and cook for 35 – 40 minutes.

6. Slice the lemon and pop one slice on top of each chicken breast with a sprig of fresh parsley.

Top Tip:

"Whenever I make this dish, everyone just can't get enough. Paul's its biggest fan! The good news is you can prepare it 4 days in advance if you want to serve it cold for a buffet. If you want to use a larger piece of gammon just boil it for longer. That's the most important part, as it tenderises the meat so it just melts in the mouth. I like to serve it hot as a Sunday roast with all the trimmings. Enjoy!"

Dee's Gammon with Sherry

Ingredients

625g (approx. 1/3 joint smoked gammon)
12 black peppercorns
6 bay leaves (fresh or dried)
200ml (7 fl oz) sweet sherry
2 tbsp light brown sugar

Method

1. Put the gammon, leaving the string around it and the rind on, in a large saucepan.

2. Add the peppercorns and the bay leaves.

3. Pour over enough boiling water to cover the gammon.

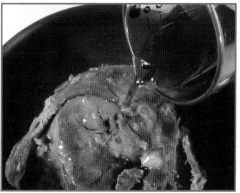

4. Bring back to the boil on the hob, then leave on a high simmer for two hours. Keep topping the pan up with boiling water (I know it's a long time but trust me its worth it!)

5. After the two hours have passed, pre-heat the oven to 225°C / gas mark 7.

6. Remove the gammon from the saucepan. Cut the string off and remove the rind. Discard the bay leaves and peppercorns.

7. Place the gammon in an ovenproof dish and pour the sherry over.

8. Finally sprinkle the sugar over the top of the meat

9. Place in the oven for 35 - 45 minutes or until the sugar has melted. Baste in the sauce a couple of times during cooking.

10. Remove from the oven and leave to rest for 10 minutes.

11. Carve the gammon into thin slices and spoon over the sherry and sugar sauce.

Top Tip:

"Serve in a fresh, soft bun with salad and homemade chips. So nice! As a variation try using minced chicken, turkey, lamb or pork and add a tablespoon of oats to the mixture. Also try some different flavourings, such as a tablespoon of Sweet Chilli, BBQ, Garlic and Herb, Mexican or Mint and Rosemary from the "Shake it Up!" range"

Burgers

Ingredients

400g (14 oz) minced beef
1 egg
1 onion (finely chopped)
1 tbsp plain flour
Salt and pepper

Method

1. Simply mix all the ingredients together thoroughly.

2. Make into 4 good-sized burgers.

3. Either grill, or fry in a pan.

Top Tip:
"Great for a snack in a hurry. Make up the omelette and wrap in greaseproof paper and eat on the go."

Omelette with Various Fillings

Ingredients

Basic Omelette

3 eggs

2 tbsp milk/cream or Soya milk/water.

Salt and pepper

Method

1. Lightly oil and pre-heat a non-stick pan.

2. Gently beat the ingredients together and pour into the hot pan.

3. Swirl the mixture round and then allow it to settle. As it cooks around the edges, draw the edges into the centre, allowing the raw egg to set around the outside again.

4. Do this until it has nearly set then add your favourite filling.

5. Fold over and allow to cook through. The milk, cream or other liquid in the mixture creates steam causing the omelette to puff up.

6. Serve and eat straight away.

Of course, you can cook this in an omelette maker if you have one.

Different filling ideas:

Broccoli and cooked tuna
Breakfast Omelette with bacon, sausage and mushrooms
Spanish Omelette with cooked potato and fried onion
Hotdogs and onions
Tomato
Fried mushrooms (various types)
Spinach
Ham and cheese (Gruyere is good!)
Peppers and cooked chicken
Mixed herbs
Pepperoni
Prawn, salmon and dill, topped with cream cheese

Smoked haddock
Cooked pork and apple with Stilton cheese
Cooked lamb and mint
Cooked chicken livers
Fried leeks with onions and grated cheese
Sun-dried tomatoes chopped roasted peppers
Asparagus omelette topped with hot mayonnaise sauce
Smoked salmon with triple cheese (Cheddar, Red Leicester and Cream Cheese)
Parma ham with asparagus
Cooked turkey and tarragon

Top Tip:

"Delicious with a jacket potato, or served with a pizza or salad"

Try varying the recipe by adding some of the following: -
Sultanas or raisins
Curry powder
Walnuts
Chopped or sliced apple
Mandarins
Beetroot
Prawns
Sweetcorn
Grapes
Pineapple

Coleslaw

Ingredients
½ a white cabbage
4 carrots (peeled)
1 large onion (peeled)
5 tbsp mayonnaise
Salt and pepper

Method

1. Slice the cabbage finely in a food processor with the slicing blade attachment.

2. Do the same with the onion.

3. Change the blade to a grater for the carrots.

4. Place all the prepared vegetables into a bowl and add the mayonnaise.

5. Season to taste.

6. Mix well, chill and serve.

You can also use a vinaigrette dressing instead of mayonnaise.

Top Tip: (Roux)

"You can add a nice strong Cheddar to make a sauce for cauliflower cheese, or to top a lasagne. For a mousaka add some grated nutmeg. Try fried bacon and onion in a pastry flan case, with the sauce poured over the top and bake in the oven. Great with chicken and mushrooms as a pie filling, or with chicken and white wine cooked in the oven and served with rice"

Top Tip: (All In One)

"This sauce is just so easy and goes very well with fish, however you can leave out the dill and add what you want to it. Below are just a few ideas to start you off:

Parsley
Cheese
Fried onions
Breadcrumbs
   (for easy bread sauce)
Mixed herbs

You can even make your own rum or brandy sauce with it for Christmas. Just leave out the salt, pepper and dill and add caster sugar to taste, then rum or brandy and cream. Whatever's your favourite tipple!

Basic White Sauce with Dill
All In One method and Roux method

Ingredients
(All in one method)
25g (1 oz) plain flour
40g (1 ½ oz) butter
425ml (¾ pint) milk
Salt and pepper to taste
Dried dill

Ingredients
(Roux method)
25g (1 oz) butter
25g (1 oz) plain flour
275ml (½ pint) milk
Salt and pepper to taste
1 small onion (peeled and chopped in half)

Method

1. Place all the ingredients, apart from the dill, into a saucepan.

2. Heat over a medium heat, whisking all the ingredients together continuously, until the sauce begins to thicken.

3. Turn the heat to its lowest setting and let the sauce cook for 7 minutes, giving the occasional stir to make sure it does not stick.

4. At the end of the cooking time, stir in the dill.

Method

This is a basic onion flavour, roux based sauce.

1. Place the onion and milk in a saucepan and warm to just below boiling point.

2. Melt the butter in another saucepan on a gentle heat.

3. Add the flour, mixing all the time and allow to cook out for two minutes.

4. Next, slowly add the warm flavoured milk to the flour and butter mixture, a little at a time, straining out the onion. (The reason you add the milk warm, is because if it were cold it would harden the butter making your sauce lumpy).

5. Stir all the time to keep the sauce smooth.

6. Bring to the boil, still stirring all the time and then simmer for 5 minutes.

7. Season to taste.

Top Tip:

"This salad takes minutes to prepare and tastes amazing. If you want to make a different version of it, just leave out the fruit and nuts and add cooked prawns, dill, chives and just squeeze over some lemon juice. You can even add smoked salmon if you feel decadent!

Nut and Fruit Rice Salad

Ingredients

300g (approx. 2 cups) easy cook rice

5 spring onions

110g (4 oz) cashew nuts

50g (2 oz) salted peanuts

2 tbsp mayonnaise

1 small tin of mandarin orange segments

Freshly ground black pepper to taste

Method

1. Cook the rice as directed on the pack.

2. When the rice is cooked, drain into a colander and run under cold water until completely cooled. Leave to drain well.

3. Peel and finely chop the spring onions.

4. Open and drain the mandarin orange segments.

5. Transfer the rice into large bowl and add the spring onions, mandarins, nuts and then season with black pepper.

6. Finally add the mayonnaise. Mix well and check the seasoning.

7. Keep in the fridge overnight to allow all the flavours to mingle.

Top Tip:
 "This salad is a lovely dish to serve at any time, however if you chose, you can serve it hot with crusty bread. All you have to do is leave out the mayonnaise, keep the pasta hot and mix everything together. Top with grated Parmesan cheese. Ensure you make plenty. It's very moreish!"

Bacon and Mushroom Pasta Salad

Ingredients

250g (9 oz) conchiglie pasta (shells)
50g (2 oz) butter
25ml (1 fl oz) olive oil
1 small punnett closed cap mushrooms (sliced)
1 pack smoked streaky bacon (sliced into small strips)
A handful fresh chives (finely chopped)
A handful fresh parsley (finely chopped)
2 tbsp mayonnaise
Salt and freshly ground black pepper

Method

1. Cook the pasta according to the instructions on the pack.

2. When the pasta is cooked, place in a colander and run under cold water until completely cooled and then drain well.

3. Melt the butter and olive oil in a large frying pan. Add the sliced bacon and fry until crispy.

4. Remove the bacon from the pan and drain on kitchen paper.

5. Place the sliced mushrooms in the same frying pan and fry on a high heat until they turn golden brown and absorb all the butter and oil. (The mushrooms should look slightly charred, but not burnt.)

6. Remove the mushrooms from the pan and drain on kitchen paper.

7. Place the drained pasta in a large mixing bowl and add the bacon, mushrooms and finely chopped herbs.

8. Then add the mayonnaise, salt and black pepper. Stir together well and check the seasoning.

9. Cover and place in fridge for at least two hours.

Top Tip:
    "You can add different things to this tasty salad. Try cooked bacon or ham. Once again, this dish always tastes better after one day in the fridge. It gives the flavours time to merge together"

Homemade Potato Salad

Ingredients

700g (1½ lb) washed small new potatoes
1 onion
1 bunch fresh chives, chopped (or one tbsp of dried chives)
2 tbsp mayonnaise
Salt and freshly ground black pepper to taste

Method

1. In a large pan, boil the potatoes in salted water until they are tender.

2. Drain the potatoes and allow them to cool.

3. Finely slice and fry the onion in a little butter, until soft and slightly caramelised. Leave to cool.

4. When the potatoes are completely cold, slice in half and add the chives and fried onions.

5. Finally stir in the mayonnaise and add salt and pepper to taste.

Top Tip:

"This recipe is very tasty indeed and takes minutes to prepare, but why not try something different"

Use the basic mixture as above and try adding ideas from the list below: -

Walnuts
Cooked leeks
Orange or lemon zest
Cooked cranberries
Sausage meat
Chestnuts
Sultanas
Red onions

Homemade Sage and Onion Stuffing

Ingredients

1 large onion
5 tbsp fresh white breadcrumbs
1 egg
2 tbsp suet (you can use vegetarian if you choose)
1 tbsp sage chopped (you can use dried if you can't get fresh)
1 tsp mixed dried herbs

Method

1. Peel and cut the onion in half. Place into a food processor and pulse for 30 seconds.

2. Add the breadcrumbs and suet. Pulse for another 10 seconds.

3. Transfer the mixture into a mixing bowl and stir in all the herbs.

4. Beat the egg in a separate bowl.

5. Add the beaten egg a little at a time to the stuffing mixture. Don't let the stuffing get mushy, but if it does don't worry, just add a few more breadcrumbs.

6. At this stage you can make stuffing balls, or stuff a turkey or chicken.

7. If you decide to cook the stuffing separately or in balls, bake for about half an hour at 200°C / gas mark 5.

The stuffing freezes very well and will keep for up to 3 months.

Top Tip:

"When serving, it's great to put a thick, sweet balsamic dressing around the outside of the plate. Serve with Parmesan shavings on the top of the risotto, accompanied by a green salad. You can substitute the chicken for raw prawns or a selection of different mushrooms and finish off with truffle oil. Use only a little, as this has a really strong flavour and is not to everyone's taste"

Chicken Risotto with Cream Cheese

Ingredients

200g (7 oz) Arborio rice
8 chicken fillets (cut into cubes)
1 large onion (chopped)
½ pt white wine
½ pt chicken stock

2 tsp chopped mixed herbs
1 tub cream cheese with garlic and herbs
1 tbsp oil
1 pack baby asparagus
110g (4 oz) sliced mushrooms

Method

1. Place the oil in a large, hot pan and fry the onions without colouring them.

2. Add the chicken and fry for 5 minutes, then add the rice, white wine, stock, mixed herbs and mushrooms.

3. Bring to the boil and simmer and stir for 15 minutes until the stock and wine have been absorbed and the rice is tender.

4. Mix in the baby asparagus. The heat from the rice will cook it in two minutes.

5. Add the cream cheese and stir. Serve piping hot.

Top Tip:

"Serving ideas: Sweet - lemon and sugar, oranges with orange liqueur and brown sugar, jam, fresh fruit. Savoury - chicken in a creamy sauce, cheese, beef in black bean sauce, chicken with satay sauce, curried stir-fry vegetables. There are no limits!"

Top Tip:

"I've used this method for many years and it has never let me down. It's quick, easy and tastes fab! If you want to make toad in the hole, just pre-cook the sausages with some chopped onions in the oven first, then add the batter. Always make sure the batter is cold and the oil is hot and you really can't go wrong"

Pancakes and Yorkshire Puddings

Ingredients
Pancake Mix
200g (7 oz) plain flour
2 eggs
500ml (18 fl oz) milk
Pinch of salt

Ingredients
Easy Yorkshire Puddings
250ml (9 fl oz) milk
100ml (4 fl oz) water
2 eggs
125g (4 ½ oz) plain flour
Pinch of salt
1 tbsp of vegetable or sunflower oil

Method *(Pancake Mix)*

1. Mix the flour, salt, eggs and milk together to form a smooth batter. You can do this in a food processor, or in a bowl with a stick blender or hand whisk.

2. Place a little oil in a non-stick pan and wipe round with kitchen towel.

3. Heat the pan to a medium heat and place enough batter mix to thinly cover the base of pan.

4. Cook until the underside of the pancake is golden brown, then flip over and cook the other side.

Method *(Easy Yorkshire Puddings)*

1. Start by placing a large, glass measuring jug or a mixing bowl on a tea towel. (This stops it sliding about).

2. Crack the eggs into the jug or bowl and add the water.

3. With an electric whisk, beat on the highest setting for 30 seconds.

4. Then add the milk and whisk for a 1 minute on the highest setting.

5. Add the flour and salt and whisk on a medium setting for a further minute.

6. Once all the batter has been blended together, cover with cling film and place in the fridge for at least 1 hour.

7. When you are ready to cook the Yorkshire puddings, pre heat the oven to 225°C/gas mark 7.

8. Place a little oil in the container that you have chosen to use and place it in the oven for at around 10 minutes or until the oil is smoking hot.

9. Remove the batter from the fridge and give it a good stir.

10. Pour the batter into the hot container (there should be a sizzle as you do this) and bake for 35 minutes or until the puddings have risen and are golden brown.

Top Tip:

"I like my meat well done, however if you like yours medium, just adjust the roasting time for the duck. The sauce is quick and easy to make and as with most of our recipes you can make it a day in advance to save you time. This dish goes well with any vegetable you may want to serve. If you choose to, you can roast a whole duck for a festive occasion. Please don't waste the oil that comes out of the duck. Try roasting potatoes in it. Delicious!"

Duck Breasts with Easy Cherry Sauce

Ingredients

4 duck breasts
1 tin black cherry pie filling
1 large glass red wine
Zest a large orange
1 tbsp balsamic vinegar
Freshly ground black pepper to taste
1 tsp cornflour

Method

1. Pre heat the oven to 180°C / gas mark 4.

2. Start by putting your largest frying pan on the hob on a medium heat.

3. Fry the duck breasts, skin side down for 3 minutes.

4. Turn the duck over and fry for a further 3 minutes.

5. Remove the duck breasts and place them on a rack in a baking tray. (The grill pan is a great substitute if you havn't got a baking tray with a rack). Place in the oven for 45 minutes.

6. Place the pie filling in a large saucepan and heat to simmering point, then add the red wine, leaving a little in the glass to mix with the cornflour later.

7. Add the balsamic vinegar to the pan and bring up to the boil.

8. Mix the cornflour with the remainder of the wine and pour into the pan.

9. Add the orange zest and black pepper.

10. Turn the heat down to a simmer and cook for 6 minutes or until the sauce has thickened. It should just coat the back of a metal spoon.

11. Take the duck out of the oven and let it rest for 10 minutes.

12. Serve this dish by pouring little of the sauce over the duck and garnish with orange slices if you wish.

Top Tip:

"Serve hot with new potatoes and coleslaw, or cold at a picnic or buffet. Change the bacon and onion for different fillings such as leek, asparagus, mushrooms, sun-dried tomatoes, Parma ham, tuna, French beans, sausage or spring onions. Line the base of the quiche with tomato sauce and mixed herbs first and then pour the filling on top"

Bacon and Onion Quiche

Ingredients

Shortcrust Pastry
200g (7 oz) plain flour
110g (4 oz) cold butter (cut into cubes)
A little water
Pinch of salt

Filling
100ml (4 fl oz) whole milk
50ml (2 fl oz) cream
4 eggs
150g (5 oz) grated mature cheddar cheese
5 rashers bacon (smoked is best)
1 large onion (sliced)
1 large tomato (sliced)
Salt and pepper

Method

1. Make the shortcrust pastry by putting the flour, butter and salt into a food processor. Blitz until it looks like fine breadcrumbs and then add some water, a little at a time until a dough is formed, which leaves the sides of the mixing bowl clean.

2. If possible, allow the dough to rest the fridge for 30 minutes wrapped in cling film.

3. Roll out the pastry and line a nine-inch flan ring.

4. Prick the base of the pastry case with a fork.

5. Lightly beat the eggs and use a little to glaze the base of the pastry. (This helps to stop it going soggy).

6. Bake in the oven for ten minutes at 180°C/gas mark 4 - this is known as "baking blind"

7. Fry the onions and bacon in a little oil and then add to the pastry case.

8. Sprinkle the grated cheese over the bacon and onions.

9. Beat the eggs, milk and cream together, then season with salt and pepper.

10. Pour into the filled flan case and place slices of tomato on the top.

11. Bake at 190°C/gas mark 5, for 30 to 40 minutes until firm and golden brown.

Top Tip:
"Serve with creamy mashed potatoes and steamed vegetables. Wow! This is good when you're hungry and it's a great way of getting iron in your diet. There's enough here for six servings"

Liver and Bacon

Ingredients

500g (18 oz) liver (sliced thinly)
3 tbsp plain flour
6 rashers bacon
2 onions (peeled and sliced)
2 tbsp oil
250ml (9 fl oz) beef stock (made with 2 stock cubes)
1 tbsp of Worcestershire sauce (optional)
3 shakes of soy sauce (optional)
Salt and pepper to taste

Method

1. Place the oil in a large frying pan and heat on a high setting.

2. Coat the liver with flour then fry with the bacon and onions for about 5 minutes.

3. Reduce the temperature, so as not to burn, and turn the liver from time to time to give a nice even colour.

4. Add any remaining flour and stir in.

5. Next, gradually add the stock, stirring all the time and bring up to the boil.

6. Add the Worcestershire sauce, soy sauce and check the seasoning.

7. Simmer on a low heat, covered, for 45 minutes.

Top Tip:

"Serve with a salad. Just like being back in Greece!"

Moussaka

Ingredients

300g (11 oz) minced lamb
1 onion (peeled and chopped)
1 tin plum tomatoes in juice
500g (18 oz) peeled & sliced potatoes
2 tbsp oil
1 aubergine (sliced)
Pinch cinnamon
2 Oxo cubes
1 tsp flour
Paprika and ground nutmeg
Salt and pepper to taste

Ingredients (page 79)

White sauce
(Roux method)
25g (1 oz) butter
25g (1 oz) plain flour
275ml (½ pint) milk
Salt & pepper to taste
1 small onion (peeled
and chopped in half)

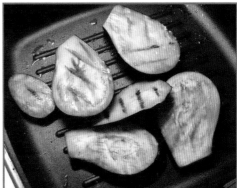

Method

1. Fry the sliced potatoes in the oil until cooked and place in bottom of an ovenproof dish.

2. Drain the plum tomatoes and save the juice. Cut the tomatoes in half and place over the potatoes.

3. Fry the aubergine slices with a little oil for 4 minutes on each side until soft and place these on top of the tomatoes.

4. Fry the mince and onions until brown and drain any excess oil.

5. Add the flour and stir in, then the pinch of cinnamon and seasoning.

6. Mix 2 tablespoons of water with the juice from the tomatoes, then crumble in the Oxo cubes and stir together with the mince, bringing the mixture to the boil.

7. Pour the mixture over the aubergines.

8. Make up the Basic White Sauce (Roux method) from Recipe 21.

9. Add a pinch of cinnamon to the sauce and pour over the mince.

10. Dust with paprika and nutmeg.

11. Bake in the oven at 190°C / gas mark 5, until golden brown on top.

Top Tip:

"Try using different fruits instead of strawberries, such as blueberries, raisins, sultanas, cherries and so on. Or, once almost frozen, place into silicone muffin moulds and fully freeze, then turn out onto a plate. Drizzle chocolate sauce round the edge of the plate and crumble chocolate flake on the top. This looks a wow if you're having a dinner party!"

Ice Creams and Sorbet

Ingredients
Strawberry Cheesecake Ice Cream
110g (4 oz) natural yoghurt
175g (6 oz) Mascarpone cheese
110g (4 oz) condensed milk
275ml (10 fl oz) double cream
110g (4 oz) digestive biscuits (broken into small pieces)
150g (5 oz) strawberries (finely chopped)

Method
1. Mix together the yoghurt, Mascarpone cheese, condensed milk and double cream in a bowl and then gently stir in the biscuits and strawberries.
2. Place in an ice cream maker, or in the freezer in a freezer-safe bowl and keep stirring every 45 minutes until fully frozen and ready to eat.

Ingredients
Bucks Fizz Sorbet
1 bottle bucks fizz
1 small tin mandarin segments drained and chopped (optional)

Method
1. Pour the bucks fizz into an ice cream maker and let the machine do its magic, or prepare in the freezer as above.
2. To make it extra special, place the chopped mandarin pieces in as well.

Ingredients
Marmalade Ice Cream
1 large tub natural yoghurt
2 tbsp (approx. 50g / 2 oz) marmalade
2 tbsp caster sugar

Method
1. Mix all the ingredients together and use an ice cream maker or the freezer method as above.

This sounds unusual, but marmalade ice cream is really fresh and great to cleanse the pallet. Most people who try it are really surprised how nice it is. Have a go!

Ingredients
Rich Coffee Mocha Ice Cream
500ml (18 fl oz) double cream
3 tbsp caster sugar
1 small Espresso coffee or ¼ cup very strong instant coffee chilled in fridge until cold
3 tbsp chocolate sauce
1 packet chocolate chips or your favourite chocolate bar broken into small pieces

Method
1. Mix all the ingredients together and use an ice cream maker or the freezer method as above.

Top Tip:

"This is also delicious with pears or apples instead of pineapple"

Basic Sponge Mix and Pineapple Upside-down Cake

Ingredients
Basic Sponge Mix
110g (4oz) self-raising flour
2 eggs (at room temperature)
110g (4oz) butter or margarine (at
        room temperature)
110g (4oz) castor sugar

Ingredients
Pineapple Upside-down Cake
3 pineapple rings
4 glace cherries
3 tsp of golden syrup
Basic sponge mix as seen on the left

Method

1. Mix all ingredients together in food mixer until well blended or in a bowl with a wooden spoon and some elbow grease!

2. Pour into a 20cm (8 inch) greased and floured baking tin or a Wonderflex mould and bake at 180°C/gas mark 4, for about 35 to 45 minutes until golden brown.

3. Check to see if it's cooked by placing a skewer into the sponge. If it comes out clean, it's done.

Method

1. Place the golden syrup in base of 20cm (8 inch) cake tin, Wonderflex mould or a frying pan that can go in the oven.

2. Next, put in the pineapple rings and then one cherry in the centre of each pineapple ring and one in the centre of the cake tin.

3. Carefully pour the cake mix on top.

4. Bake at 180°C/gas mark 4 for about 35 to 45 minutes until cooked.

5. Turn out onto a plate whilst hot and serve.

Top Tip:

"This cake can be made at least 2 to 3 months in advance and kept in an air-tight container. You can top it with marzipan and icing or just simply decorate the top with cherries and nuts. Ideal for festive occasions. It's up to you, but one thing's for sure… it's really yum!"

Dark Fruitcake

Ingredients

450g (1lb) sultanas
175g (6 oz) currants
175g (6 oz) raisins
60g (2½ oz) glace cherries
4 tbsp dark rum
250g (9 oz) plain flour
1 tsp mixed spice
250g (9 oz) butter
250g (9 oz) dark brown sugar
5 eggs
60g (2 ½ oz) walnuts (chopped)
1tsp gravy browning or 1 tblsp of black treacle
Zest 1 lemon
Zest 1 orange

Method

1. Pre-heat the oven to 150C / gas mark 2.

2. Line a 20cm (8 inch) round or 18cm (7 inch) square cake tin with greaseproof paper.

3. Place all the dried fruit in a large bowl, pour over the rum and then cover and place to one side.

4. In a mixer, cream the butter and sugar together until light and fluffy.

5. Beat the eggs in a separate bowl and add to the creamed butter and sugar mixture, a little at a time, leaving the beaters going.

6. Next add the flour, mixed spice and gravy browning or treacle, using the slowest setting on the mixer.

7. Add the glace cherries and chopped walnuts.

8. Then stir in the rum soaked fruit.

9. Finally add the lemon and orange zest.

10. Spoon the mixture into the pre-prepared tin and bake for between 3 1/2 hrs to 5 hrs depending on your oven. Test every 30 minutes after 3 1/2 hours to see if the cake is fully cooked. Test to see if the cake is fully cooked by popping a knife in the middle. If it comes out clean the cake is ready. If not don't worry, just give it a further half an hour and test again.

Top Tip:

"Delicious spread on fresh bread or used as the filling in our lemon meringue pie. Try adding some passion fruit (with or without the seeds) before cooking"

Lemon Curd

Ingredients

110g (4oz) unsalted butter
3 eggs
1 egg yolk
225g (8 oz) caster sugar
Zest three lemons
110ml (4 fl oz) lemon juice

Method

1. Melt the butter in a large bowl in the microwave on high power for 45 seconds.

2. Beat the eggs and the extra egg yolk and then pass through a sieve.

3. Whisk the sieved eggs and all the remaining ingredients together, then beat into the melted butter.

3. Cover the bowl with cling-film and pierce.

4. Return to the microwave and cook on high power for bursts of 45 seconds, then stir.

5. Repeat this stage until the mixture has thickened.

Top Tip:

*"Great served with hot custard!
Try these different fruits. - Plums,
apples, rhubarb, gooseberries,
pears, peaches and strawberries. A
combination of some of these can
work well together, like pear and apple.
Raisins or sultanas added to the soft
fruits also make a nice variation"*

Fruit Crumble

Ingredients

Crumble Topping

225g (8 oz) plain flour

110g (4 oz) butter (cold and cut into pieces)

110g (4 oz) sugar

Optional extras you can add to the basic crumble mix:-

Brown sugar instead of white

Crusts from 2 slices of brown bread

50g (2 oz) chopped walnuts (to make it extra crunchy)

Filling

700g (1 ½ lb) chosen fruit (peeled, cored, de-seeded and chopped)

60g (2 ½ oz) butter (melted)

½ tsp lemon juice (if using apples)

25g (1 oz) white or brown sugar (to taste depending on the sweetness of the fruit)

Method

1. Place all the crumble topping ingredients into a food processor and blend until the mixture resembles fine breadcrumbs. Do not over mix.

2. Place your chosen fruit in the base of an ovenproof dish (approx.1 ¼ litre).

3. Pour the melted butter over the fruit and then the sugar on top.

4. Sprinkle the crumble mixture over the fruit. Do not press down.

5. Bake for 30 to 40 minutes at 180°C / gas mark 4 until golden brown.

Top Tip:

"If you do want to make this pudding in your slow cooker, just prepare as above in the morning and cook on "low" all day (approx. 8 hours). When you walk in after a hard days work on a cold night, the smell of this cooking will really bring home the meaning of comfort food!"

Bread and Butter Pudding

Ingredients

10 slices of ready sliced, white bread

30g (1 ¼ oz) butter

60g (2 ½ oz) currants or mixed fruit

75ml (3 floz) double cream

275ml (½ pt) whole milk

110g (4 oz) caster sugar

4 eggs

The juice and zest of 1 small orange

60g (2 ½ oz) soft brown sugar

Grated nutmeg to taste

Method

1. Pre heat the oven to 180°C/gas mark 4.

2. Lightly butter a 1 litre ovenproof dish or a slow cooker.

3. Butter all the slices of bread and cut them, in half leaving the crusts on.

4. Cover the bottom of the dish with a third the bread and sprinkle half the fruit and caster sugar over the top.

5. Make another layer of bread, fruit and sugar as in step 4.

6. Use the last of the bread to cover the top.

7. In a large bowl, whisk together the milk, eggs, cream and orange juice.

8. Pour this mixture over the bread and fruit layers and allow to soak in.

9. Finally sprinkle the brown sugar, zest and grated nutmeg over the top.

10. Bake for 40 minutes until the top is golden and crunchy.

Top Tip:

"What can I say about this cheesecake? Once you have tasted it you will be hooked. The top tip I will tell you is that it really does improve with time, so I usually make it two days in advance. It's so easy, but you can pretend you spent hours slaving over it. I DO!"

I would like to dedicate this cheesecake recipe to my late father Siddy who, having tried many different recipes, said this is the best one in the whole world! Dee.

Dee's New York Cheesecake

Ingredients

300g (11 oz) chocolate chip cookies with nuts
110g (4 oz) butter
1kg (2 ¼ lb) full fat cream cheese
400g (14 oz) caster sugar
5 eggs
3 egg yolks
6 lemons
250g (9 oz) sultanas soaked in Bourbon
(Whisky will do if you have not got any Bourbon)

Method

1. Pre heat the oven to 180°C/gas mark 4.

2. Fully line a 25cm (10 inch) round spring-form cake tin with kitchen foil, as you will be baking this cheesecake in a baking tray with boiling water.

3. Melt the butter in the microwave.

4. Blitz the cookies in a processor until they are at the fine breadcrumb stage.

5. Mix the butter and cookies together and spread evenly over the base of the tin, then place in the fridge.

6. Now beat the cheese, sugar and eggs together well with an electric whisk, until the mixture is smooth.

7. Add the sultanas to the mixture.

8. Juice and zest the lemons and add to the mixture.

9. Take the tin out of the fridge and pour the mixture slowly onto the biscuit base.

10. Put the tin into a large baking tray and fill the tray with warm water so it comes half way up the side of the cake tin. PLEASE DON'T OVERFILL!

11. Bake for one hour. The cheesecake should be set, but not hard. If it feels too liquid, give it another 20 minutes until the top is a nice golden colour.

12. Once the cheesecake is cooked, remove from the tray of water and leave it to cool. Then place it into the fridge for 2 hours.

13. Gently peel away the foil and place on a serving plate.

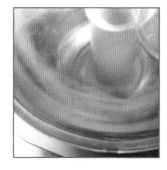  

Top Tip:
"This trifle is so easy to make and tastes fantastic! However, if you don't want to use cherries or chocolate Swiss rolls, try it with strawberries and vanilla Swiss rolls with white chocolate flakes"

Black Forest Trifle

Ingredients

2 x 240g tins black cherry pie filling
2 medium chocolate and vanilla Swiss rolls
2 tbsp cherry brandy or just brandy
275ml (½ pt) double cream
1 Flake chocolate bar

Method

1. Open the pie filling and remove nine of the cherries and wash them gently and let them dry on kitchen paper.

2. Cut the Swiss rolls into 12 pieces each.

3. Arrange half the Swiss roll slices in a glass bowl (a pretty one if possible).

4. Pour half the cherry brandy on top.

5. Empty one tin of pie filling over the Swiss roll.

6. Repeat steps 3, 4, and 5.

7. Whip the cream in a large bowl until it is light and fluffy. Not too stiff.

8. Spoon half the cream over the trifle and spread with a palette knife. Don't worry if some of the pie filling shows, as this will be covered later.

9. Put the Flake into a small plastic bag and crumble it up by rolling a rolling pin over it.

10. Sprinkle the Flake over the cream.

11. Finish whipping the cream that is left until its stiff. Place in an icing bag with a rose attachment and pipe all round the edge of the bowl and one swirl in the middle. 12. Place the cherries that you washed and saved, evenly around the trifle and pop one in the middle.

Other Smoothie Ideas:

Strawberry with ice and water. Great added to sweet white wine with a mint leaf.

Apple with water and ice.

Pear and apple with water and ice.

Raspberry and blueberry with water or milk and ice.

Kiwi, apple, blueberries with water and ice. Add a little sugar or sweetener if needed.

Banana, raspberry and oats with milk and ice.

Ice cream, berries, ice and milk.

Oranges and nectarines, water and ice.

Plums, grapes ice and water.

Peaches with yoghurt, ice, milk and oats.

Melon, grapes, ice and water.

Pineapple, mango, ice and water.

Wheatgrass powder can even be added as a great supplement!

Homemade Lemonade and Smoothies

Ingredients

Homemade Lemonade

1.5ltrs (2 ½ pts) water

5 cubes ice

1 un-waxed lemon

2 tbsp sugar or sweetener (you can vary this to your own taste)

Method

1. Place all the ingredients into a blender and mix on full power for 15seconds. No more or the lemonade will go bitter.

2. Then sieve into a jug and it's ready to serve.

Ingredients

Breakfast Smoothie

2 tbsp frozen or fresh mixed berries

1 banana

2 tbsp natural yoghurt

1 tbsp oats (helps to thicken it)

½ ltr (18 floz) milk

5 cubes ice

Method

1. Place all the ingredients into a blender on full power until smooth.

2. Serve on ice.

Top Tip:

"You can flavour the filling with lemon juice by adding it just as you end the mixing. Don't add it earlier as it could curdle. Try changing the topping to raspberries, blackberries, sliced strawberries or any other fruit of your choice"

Paul's Cheats Cheesecake

Ingredients

Base

225g (8oz) digestive biscuits
75g (3oz) butter
50g (2 oz) brown sugar

Filling

110g (4oz) natural yoghurt
1 ltr (1 ¾ pts) double cream
150g (5oz) Mascarpone cheese or soft cream cheese
110g (4oz) condensed sweetened milk

Topping

1 tin of mandarin segments

Method

1. Crush the digestive biscuits into a breadcrumb texture.

2. Melt the butter and add to the crushed biscuits and brown sugar.

3. Place into the base of a cake tin and set in the fridge.

4. Mix all the filling ingredients in a food mixer until stiff.

5. Place on top of the biscuit base and leave in the fridge for at least 2, but if possible, overnight.

6. Top with mandarin segments and garnish with a sprig of fresh mint. Wonderful!

Top Tip:

"This sauce is best served warm. You can use it for almost anything, but please try it over Paul's homemade ice cream. You won't be sorry! You can use the sauce to make a delicious chocolate tart. Buy or make a sweet shortcrust pastry case. Pour in the chocolate sauce and allow it to set in the fridge. Garnish with chocolate shavings. Also, you can use the sauce to cover a chocolate Swiss roll and make a fabulous Yule Log at a fraction of the price!"

Easy Chocolate Fudge Sauce

Ingredients

110g (4 oz) good quality plain chocolate
40g (1 ½ oz) butter
75g (3 oz) of caster sugar
75ml (3 floz) evaporated milk
55ml (2 floz) double cream

Method

1. Melt the chocolate and butter in a bowl, over a pan of just simmering water.

2. In a saucepan, dissolve the sugar in the evaporated milk and bring to the boil.

3. Once the mixture has boiled, take it off the heat and add the cream.

4. Next, take the melted butter and chocolate mix off the heat

5. Finish by combining the two mixtures together. Add the evaporated milk mix to the chocolate mix a dessertspoonful at a time and stir well.

Top Tip:

"This is such an easy dish to do and you can experiment all you like. You can add nuts, berries, peel, spices… anything you want. They really are best served hot with cream"

Baked Apples

Ingredients

450g (1 lb) cooking apples
110g (4 oz) soft brown sugar
110g (4 oz) butter
110g (4 oz) mixed fruit
1 tbsp golden syrup

Method

1. Pre heat the oven to 180°C/gas mark 4.

2. Butter a large oven dish or slow cooker.

3. Core the apples.

4. Fill the apples with the mixed fruit and sugar and place a little butter on top of each one.

5. Drizzle golden syrup over each apple.

6. Bake for 1½ hours in oven, or on "low" all day in your slow cooker.

Top Tip:

"This is a quick, cheap, chocolate and coffee mouse. If you want a darker colour, then add a little gravy browning to the mixture. Gravy browning is only caramelised sugar, so it won't affect the flavour. Do not over whip the cream, as it will turn to butter!"

Coffee & Chocolate Mousse and Quick Fruit Mousse

Ingredients

Coffee and Chocolate Mousse

1 ltr (1 ¾ pts) double cream

3 tbsp chocolate sauce

1 tsp coffee powder (mix with a little hot water first and cool)

2 tsp sugar or sweetener

50g (2 oz) chocolate chips or a crumbled Flake

Method

1. Whisk the double cream in a food mixer until it starts to thicken.

2. Once starting to thicken, add the chocolate sauce, coffee mixture, sugar and chocolate pieces. Continue to whisk.

3. When thickened, spoon into dishes and place in the fridge to set.

4. Serve with grated chocolate on the top.

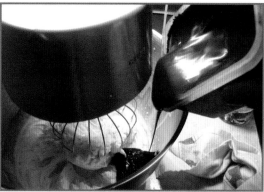

Ingredients

Quick Fruit Mousse

1 ltr (1 ¾ pts) double cream

150g (5 oz) frozen berries of your choice (allow to defrost slightly)

3 tbsp castor sugar or sweetener

Method

1. Whisk the double cream in a food mixer until it starts to thicken.

2. Once starting to thicken, add the fruit and sugar. Continue to whisk.

3. When thickened, spoon into dishes and place in the fridge to set.

4. Serve with fresh berries

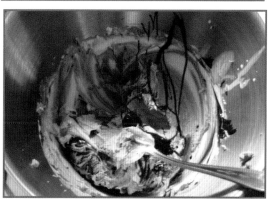

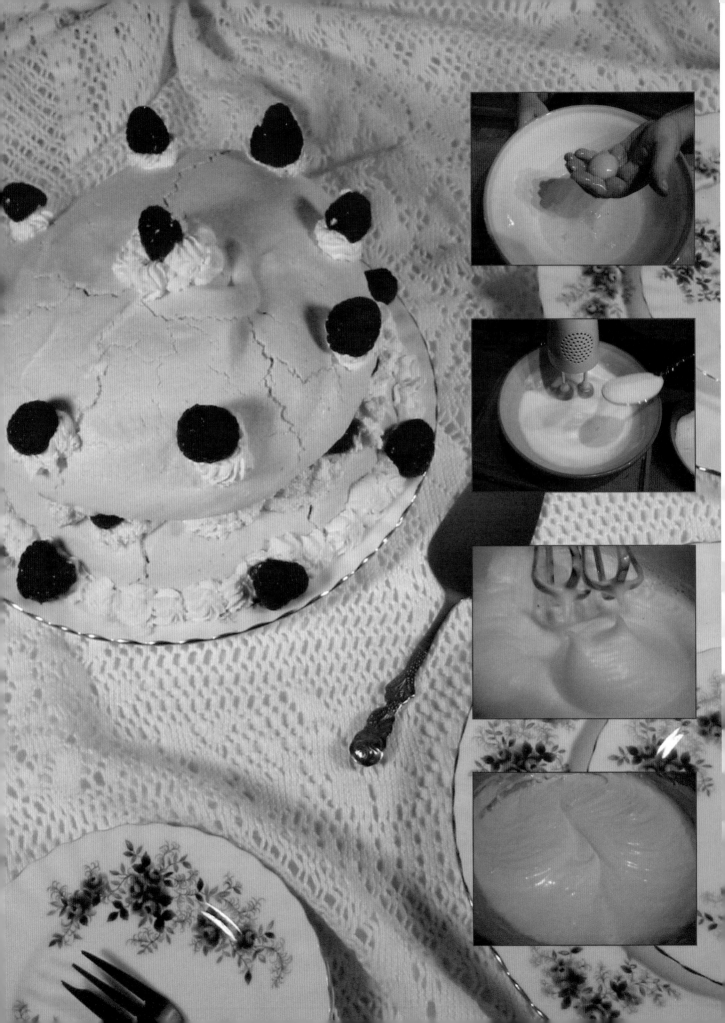

Pavlova and Meringues

Ingredients
Whites of 6 large eggs
75g (3 oz) caster sugar
Lemon juice

Method

1. Pre heat the oven to 150°C/gas mark 2.

2. Line two, flat oven trays with non-stick paper or use a silicone baking sheet.

3. Wipe a large bowl with lemon juice and dry with kitchen paper. Repeat with the whisks you are going to use.

4. Separate the eggs and place the egg whites in the clean bowl.

5. Whisk the egg whites on a medium speed for 30 seconds, then turn the whisk up to full speed and continue to whisk until they form soft peaks.

6. Now start to add the sugar, a little at a time.

7. Once all the sugar is added, the mixture should be smooth and glossy.

8. Use a large spoon and place half the mixture on each tray. Spread into a circle about 20cm (8 inches) across, but don't spread it too thinly.

9. Place in the oven and turn the oven down to 140°C/gas mark 1.

10. Bake for one hour then turn the oven off, leaving the meringues in for at least 8 hours to dry out.

11. Fill as below in Top Tips.

Top Tips
    "Once you have cooked your meringues you can fill them with whatever you like. My favourite is raspberries and cream, however you just use your imagination. Below are a few ideas to start you off:

Kiwi and mandarins, strawberries and mint, pineapple, mango and cream, Paul's chocolate mousse, crème fraiche and grapes, mixed berries and Greek yoghurt.

If you want to make small meringues, just use the same method, but place one tablespoonful of mixture for each meringue on the baking trays. Bake as above and then top with a teaspoonful of fruit and cream. Go on, have a go! "

Top Tip:

"You can serve this tasty treat hot or cold. If you feel like a real change, try exchanging Paul's lemon curd for orange curd. Mmm... delicious! If you want to make a Baked Alaska, place some sponge in the base of a dish and sprinkle with sweet sherry. Place a block of ice cream on the sponge, then cover completely with the meringue mix. Bake in a hot oven at 220ºC/gas mark 7 for 10 minutes, or until the meringue starts to go golden brown. Serve immediately"

Lemon Meringue Pie

> **Ingredients**
> Your own shortcrust pastry OR buy a pack
> of ready rolled OR buy a sweet pie case
> 1 jar Paul's homemade lemon curd
> 5 egg whites
> 110g (4 oz) caster sugar
> A little butter

Method

1. Pre heat the oven to 190°C/gas mark 5.

2. Use a round pie dish, about 15cm (6 inches) across and butter well.

3. Lay the pastry in the pie dish making sure you cover the rim of the dish.

4. Prick the base of the pastry with a fork.

5. Bake blind for 20 minutes.

6. Take the pastry out of the oven and turn the oven down to 150°C / gas mark 2.

7. Pour the lemon curd into the pastry shell.

8. Make the meringue as directed in the Pavlova recipe.

9. Spread the meringue mixture over the curd.

10. Place back in the oven and cook for 45 minutes, until the meringue is crisp on the outside and gooey inside.

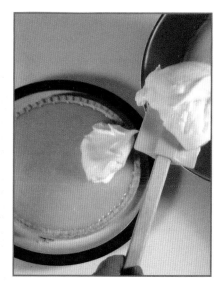

Notes...

...notes

AFTERWORD

They say, "all good things must come to an end", but in this case that's far from true. This is only the beginning…

As we said in the foreword, we wanted this cookbook to be different, and to be a book for all the family. We hope that we've succeeded in our mission and that you enjoyed trying out our recipes, as much as Paul and I did creating them.

The creation of this book and the recipes was truly a labour of love and a family affair. Everything was cooked in Paul's own kitchen and his living room was turned into a photographic studio for the pictures! Even the crockery and cutlery we used were our own. We had lots of help from family and friends, whether it was washing up or chopping vegetables, so we would like to thank one and all for their support.

"It's a serious business this cookery book writing lark you know!"

A special thank you goes to Miller brothers, David and Simon, for their expert photographic and layout skills – we're proud to have them on our team.

By the way, I'd like to quote a couple of things said while we were having dinner one night in Paul's kitchen, with some of our helpers and friends. We'd just come to the end of a hard day's work, preparing the last of the dishes for the book - so you can imagine what the kitchen looked like - when Jeff said:

"You know what? You could play "I Spy" for a MONTH in Paul's kitchen and never run out of things to guess!"

Paul said of Andrew's help, *"He made Cinderella look work-shy!"*

Now it's your turn to let us know what you think. Please do get in touch and ask Paul or I any questions you may have.

Feel free to write to us at:

**Paul Brodel,
PO Box 1,
Harston
Cambridge,
CB22 7PX**

Email us on:

cook@paulbrodel.co.uk

visit our web address at:

www.paulbrodel.co.uk

We really want to know how much you enjoyed the recipes and remember, this is Volume 1. - you could be featured in Volume 2.

All we need in the first instance is the recipe you would like to submit along with your name and daytime telephone number. Good luck!

We look forward to hearing from you and thank you for purchasing this book.

Paul & Dee.

"Food? Let ME help!!"

"It's not ALL work, work, work!"

P.S Would you like to be kept informed of any new recipes, public appearances and special offers from Paul and Dee? Then please write to us, email us or go to the website and register.

INDEX A-Z

A big thank you to...

"Kitchen Aids"

For their tough machines working behind the scenes, mixing, kneading and whisking.

"Shake It Ups"

For giving us such amazing flavours in the convenience of a bottle.

"Oxo"

For adding great flavour to our dishes for so many years.

"Freshpods"

For helping our fruit and vegetables to last so much longer, hence saving money.

"Kenwood"

For their quality, electrical kitchen equipment, saving so much preparation time.

"Palson"

For their amazing products (griddle, wok and multi-cooker) which speed up cooking time and save energy.

"Meyer"

For their extensive range of cookware, which is so durable and easy to clean.

"Berghoff"

For the versatility and food release capability of their products from oven to table.